Changing Your Life Through Positive Thinking: How To Overcome Negativity and Live Your Life To The Fullest

Jennifer N. Smith

Copyright and Disclaimer

CONTENTS

**Changing Your Life Through
Positive Thinking: How To
Overcome Negativity and
Live Your Life To The Fullest**
Introduction   1

Positive Thinking Q & A   4

**Part One: Positive Thinking
and How It Can Change Your
Life**

1   What Is Positive Thinking?   7

2   What Is Negativity?   12

3   Stress and Anxiety   21

4   Circling Thoughts   28

**Part Two: How To Become A   33
Positive Thinker**

6   Habits Of The Positive Person   39

7   How Do You Talk To Yourself?   43

8	Physical and Mental Benefits of Humor	52
9	Cutting Out Toxic People	56
10	Holding Yourself Accountable For How You Think	62
11	Letting Go Of Control	65
12	You Can't Change Others – Only Yourself	68
13	How to Stop Worrying and Be Happier	72
14	How To Believe In Yourself	78
15	How To Practice Self Soothing	83
16	Radical Steps Toward Self-Empowerment Through Positive Thinking	87
17	Conclusion	91

Introduction

Some people seem to think that the power of positive thinking is just a bunch of mumbo-jumbo. **A lot of people don't understand just how much we are able to influence our own brains and impact our lives for the better**. Although this is a difficult concept to wrap our heads around a lot of the time, most of us are willing to do our best to stay positive because we just seem to understand that it does great things for our bodies and minds.

If you are worried that your life is being negatively impacted by a lack of positive thinking, then you are probably right. Reading this book is going to help you to understand all of the power that lies in positivity, and how easy it can be for us to change our perspective and ultimately improve our health, along with virtually every other aspect of our lives. The power of positive thinking is not just in the heads of hippies and therapists, **there is actually scientific evidence that proves that thinking positively can impact us for the best.**

1

All of us make mistakes in our thinking, this is a common aspect of human nature. However, unless we are able to take the steps we need in order to correct our mistakes, then we may stay stuck and doomed to a life that is not fulfilling us in every way possible.

If you would like to learn more about how positive thinking can change your mindset for the better, reading this book will introduce you to some key concepts that can completely alter the way you perceive your own life. By empowering yourself with the knowledge that we can accrue from thinking positively, then you are giving yourself the key to a happier and healthier life. All of us make mistakes in our thinking, this is a common aspect of human nature. However, unless we are able to take the steps we need in order to correct our mistakes, then we may stay stuck and doomed to a life that is not fulfilling us in every way possible.

You are going to learn everything from what positive thinking really means, how to avoid negative thinking, the health and scientific benefits of positive thinking, how stress and anxiety can affect us on a daily journey as we attempt to undergo a path of positivity, and battling negative thoughts that prevent us from thinking positively to all of the ways that we may be sabotaging our own positive thinking and what we can do to change it. **The culmination of this knowledge will equip us with everything we need to change our lives forever.**

By following this advice, people who have a difficult time thinking positively may find themselves learning faster than ever about how they may be able to change their lives and improve their health simply by changing the way they see the world around them. We have a lot more power over our happiness then we generally believe we do, and until we are able to truly take that fact into our own hands and attempt to convey what we believe to be true and positive, we may stay stuck in a vicious cycle that prevents us from growing and can even cause more stress and health problems then we need.

So don't wait. Start now and discover for yourself how you can change your life to positive thinking and overcome the obstacles to your happiness so that you can remove negativity and live a longer and healthier life today!

Positive Thinking Q & A

Q: What is positive thinking and how does it work?

A: Positive thinking is a way to change your mindset from being negative to positive so that we can begin to believe that our lives are more within our control. It is a total shift in perspective that can allow us to change our lives and improve our health and well-being. Negativity is a slow killer, while positivity can help us to improve our longevity and stay happier and healthier for a long time.

Q: Is it really possible for us to change how we think?

A: Yes, of course it is! If we are dedicated to our task and we stay diligent, there is nothing about our perceptions that we can't change. Even if it seems difficult, this is mostly because of the physical addiction our brains have to our negative feelings. The book will cover more of this concept in depth later.

Q: How long does it take to become a positive thinker?

A: They say that to break a habit, it can take up to 21 days. If you would like to change your mindset and you follow some of the advice and techniques outlined in the book, you may want to give yourself a good month or two before you see the tremendous results that come quickly and easily as the result of training yourself in order to think more positively in a natural way.

Q: What if you have had really bad experiences and you don't know how to change them?

A: mindfulness is one important technique that many positive thinkers utilized today. Mindfulness allows us to stay in the present moment and avoid associations to the past that made the present moment feel more overwhelming than it needs to be. Mindfulness will be discussed further in the book. Some people may even turn to alternative therapies in order to help them process their past and stay focused on a more positive future. The advice in this book will surely help either way.

Q: Is there a downside to positive thinking?

A: The downside to positive thinking is that if you don't know how to handle your negative emotions, because everyone will deal with negative emotions at some point, you may be prone to a meltdown more powerful and intense than you might anticipate. It's important to learn how to properly release your negativity into the world so that you are not unleashing it on innocent people. This will be covered in another chapter.

Q: How does positive thinking really work?

A: Positive thinking works because it can help us to rewire the neural pathways in our brains so that we are no longer addicted to negative emotions and thoughts. It can help us to change our perspective on new situations so that we are not plagued by stress and anxiety, but rather excited by the joy of new possibilities.

Part One: Positive Thinking And How It Can Change Your Life

Chapter 1: What is Positive Thinking?

Most of us have already heard of positive thinking, and it seems pretty self-explanatory. However, it is a lot more complex than it might seem. Positive thinking entails a large amount of work before it can truly begin to change your life. But I think this work is fun work, and it can be easy work. It is worth it and it leaves us feeling great about ourselves and the direction that we are going in. Without this kind of work, it is impossible for us to move forward in our lives without any inhibitions.

Most of us have a difficult time allowing ourselves to let go of the past and surrender our negativity to the universe. We feel more in control if we put the negativity up front, **because for some reason we believe that the negativity can protect us somehow from the pains of our lives.**

Unfortunately, this isn't true. Negativity actually causes us a lot of grief. Especially using it as a defense mechanism. Although it can seem to give us more power in a situation or

dynamic, this power has not been earned and it can quickly sour our relationships. Thinking positively is a way to help us to empower ourselves and provide us with the motivation we need to successfully pursue our own peace of mind.
Everybody has got a difficult life situation to cope with, and if you are finding yourself plagued with negativity and unable to discover the joys that can reward our lives when we think positively, then you are in serious need of a brain makeover.

Positive thinking can only start with us. It is not something that other people can do for us. We are the ones who have to do the work to train our brains to think more positively so that we can believe that we can do anything. It takes a large amount of self-discipline to get to where we want to be in life, and if we are unable to be self-starters and do things that we don't necessarily want to do or get benefited for right away, then it can be extremely frustrating for all of the parties involved when you are not going in the direction that you feel you should be going.

A great definition of positive thinking is to say that positive thinking is the act of learning how to let go of negativity so that we are able to move forward without anything weighing us down. We will be able to see the good sides and the bad sides of any given situation, and not just be overwhelmed by the negativity of the bad. Positive thinking will provide us with the help we need in order to move forward so that we do not feel as if everything in the world is awful.

Positive thinking can only start with us. It is not something that other people can do for us.

We are the ones who have to do the work to train our brains to think more positively so that we can believe that we can do anything.

When we switch our minds to a state of positive thinking, we begin to realize that there are far more blessings in our lives than there are curses. We are not alone in our suffering, and most of the time the bad things that happened to us do hurt, but they are not the be-all and end-all of our lives. They can affect us for a long time, and even if we begin to change our perspective and become positive thinkers, sometimes we are still triggered into sadness or anger because of past events. However, through the power of positive thinking, we are going to be able to isolate these events and examine them from a healthy perspective rather than in a way that affects us in the here and now.

Positive thinking helps us to move forward and examine what is right about our lives and appreciate that, rather than being miserable about what might be wrong. With the help of positive thinking, we will empower ourselves to begin to work on the things that we find negative about our lives and come to a constructive and satisfying conclusion about them.

If we are affected by something negative on a daily basis, the most we can do is either remove ourselves from the situation or change our perspective about it.

That is what positive thinking can help us to do.

We can either work on the negative things and turn them into positive things, or we can accept that the negative is negative and leave it at that. We don't have to think any more about it. **If we are affected by something negative on a daily basis, the most we can do is either remove ourselves from the situation or change our perspective about it. That is what positive thinking can help us to do.**

If we are not able to keep our minds focused on the positive, most of the time the bad things become even bigger and

better than they need to be. There is no balance, and the
weight of the bad things makes the good things seem very
small. We stopped losing sight of what we should be grateful
for and instead focus on the things that we want and don't
have. This can completely ruin your life, especially when you
have a difficult time believing that there is anything positive
to look forward to in the world.

Positive thinking can bring us a great amount of joy, and it
can help us to avoid the dangers and pitfalls of being trapped
in a cycle of negativity. It's extremely important for
everybody to learn how to manage the negative feelings and
focus on appreciating the positive aspects of our lives.
Nothing can help us more out of any situation and staying
open to new possibilities and opportunities. Being stuck in a
negative mindset can cause us to completely miss out on
things that could have made our lives that much better.

Chapter 2: What Is Negativity?

Every one of us suffers from negativity at some point or another in our lives. Negativity is something that most of us would prefer to avoid, but unfortunately that can be very difficult. Everybody is an individual person, and these problems can persist whether we are all thinking positively or not. Each of us has our own perspective and opinion on things, and conflict is bound to occur one way or another.

Despite this, negativity does have its place in the world and it is important for us to learn how to handle it so that we can move forward in our journey of positive thinking. The best way to do this is to learn about it and understand negativity the best that we can, along with discovering new methods of processing our negative emotions so that we can begin a journey toward a healthier life.

Negativity generally abounds when we are presented with thoughts or feelings that make us feel badly. Negative thoughts can be very powerful, because sometimes they are very rational and hard to discount. If you can't disprove the negative feelings, and they just feel even more solidified and think they have a right to be there. Most people turn their negative feelings into a source of power because the negative feelings seem to be more strong than positive ones. Positive things don't tend to stand the test of time. They seem to fall apart rather quickly and leave us feeling worse than if we had never had them at all. For this reason, many people began to suffer from depression and anxiety, believing that it is better to be sad that to take a chance on being glad and to have it taken away.

This is a very defeating attitude to have, and it can cause serious troubles throughout the rest of your life. Most people who have struggled with depression will tell you that taking a chance on the positive emotions is actually the best thing that you can ever do for yourself. There is no telling what could happen if you are willing to think positively and take the risk of becoming vulnerable to your own happiness. That is one of the bravest things that you can do, but most people hide behind their negativity, being cynics and skeptics and putting other people down because of their own unhappiness. They don't understand why they should be positive, and they don't understand how their negativity can impact other people.

Unfortunately, negativity does impact other people just as much as it can impact ourselves. If you are being a negative person, you can make a positive person feel insecure or unhappy unnecessarily. Consider painting. Whenever you want to make a grey colored paint, you will have to add a lot more white into the dark paint than you add black into the white to change the color. **Consider positivity as the white paint and negativity as the black paint. Negativity seems stronger and more all-encompassing and consuming.** It has the ability to infiltrate every aspect of our lives until we feel terrible and hopeless at times. It can cause us to give up on things before we have even started, and it can make us forget that our pile of white paint is just as big, or generally, even bigger than the pile of black paint beside it.

This is the most common difficulty that we face when we are painting, just as it is one of the most common difficulties that we face in life. The black seems stronger than the white, but the fact is that the white is stronger than the black. The good is stronger than the bad. The good has the ability to make the terrible black aspects of our lives to seem like it is nothing. The problem with this is that negativity can become very dangerous when it is not properly expressed. We all have to learn proper ways of managing our anger, and unfortunately this goes against a lot of society's teachings.

We have to keep smiling in order to maintain good relationships. That is a lie that society tells us. Everybody gets angry, and if these angers build up, it can destroy our relationships and our perspective. We have to deal with the negativity and not pretend that it isn't there. That causes dangerous problems.

If we hold onto negativity without fully processing it, when we do end up releasing it on unsuspecting people, the results can be disastrous and scary. Sometimes it can turn violent, other times it can turn loud and messy. Either way, expressing negativity after we have been holding onto it for too long is a very dangerous thing.

We tend to lose our perspective and forget how to be rational. Emotions are a lot more complex than we tend to give them credit for. Most of us are taught to believe that they are silly and needless things that we should ignore. Unfortunately, they are our driving forces, and if we do not deal with them properly, we can really ruin the relationships that we care about the most.

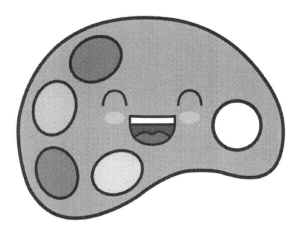

negativity does impact other people just as much as it can
impact ourselves. If you are being a negative person, you can
make a positive person feel insecure or unhappy unnecessarily.
Consider painting. Whenever you want to make a grey colored
paint, you will have to add a lot more white into the dark paint
than you add black into the white to change the color.

There are four definite types of negative thinking. Sometimes
we only affect ourselves with our negative thinking, while
other times we affect other people by thinking too negatively.
**One type of negative thinking is called
personalizing.** Many people do this, and it is pretty
common. If you are personalizing a negative experience, that
means that you believe that it has happened simply because
it is your own fault. You automatically assume that anything
bad is related to something that you have done.

This happens to a lot of people with anxiety in social
relationships, such as those that one person is not interested
in or they are busy and cannot meet up with another person.
The person who has been overlooked in the social interaction
may feel as if the person they want to out with is not going

because they have done something wrong. They assume that the responsibility is on them, and forget that the person may have a slew of their own reasons for doing what they have done. Many people who suffer from social anxiety can relate to personalizing as a negative thinking strategy.

Another type of negative thinking is catastrophizing. When you catastrophize something, that means that you assume that the worst is going to happen. Catastrophic thinkers are very anxious as well, and they have a tendency to believe that every situation may turn out to be terrible. They are not very optimistic that they do not have into new situations with a lot of these, especially when they believe that it is going to turn out to be difficult. This can also begin to affect us if one bad thing happens during the beginning of the day, and you allow it to ruin the rest of your day. You just put yourself into a catastrophic mindset, where you believe that there is nothing that will turn around the negative feeling of the day that you are experiencing.

Another form of negative thinking is called polarizing. People who have a polar mindset tends to believe that they should only view the world in terms of black and white. This can be extremely exhausting for yourself and for the other people around you. There is nothing that is only good or bad, at least not in the way that people who polarize tend to believe. A lot of people have negative self-talk that causes them to think that they are only good as long as they are perfect.

This can be extremely dangerous and can cause a lot of anxiety and stress in a person that can lead to negative thinking patterns and a lot of resentment toward the rest of the world, who they may perceive or believe that they are imperfect or to hold them to a certain standard of perfection. Polarizing is extremely dangerous and difficult for people to deal with, especially if you are in a close relationship. There is a personality disorder known as **bipolar personality** disorder that can cause this polarizing effect to impact your life at an even more extreme level. Fortunately, bipolar disorder can be dealt with and treated through the care of professionals if you fear that you may have symptoms of a bipolar disorder.

Another way that people think negatively is by filtering. Filtering means that you only look at the bad and you forget about the good things. This is one of the most common things that people do, and it can be highly dangerous for our positive state of being. If we are not able to acknowledge that good things happen alongside the bad, then we can become easily depressed and have dangerous bouts of anger and negativity toward the outside world. People who filter in this way, can be having a wonderful day and become stuck once they get one snag. One tiny hiccup can ruin the entire experience of your day, and you may find yourself feeling ultimately depressed because you are not able to seek out and appreciate the positive aspects of your experiences.

Fortunately, there are a lot of great ways that we can deal with our negative emotions, despite their complexities. First of all, it can be helpful if we stop having a doomed mentality. Most of us like to pick at our negative emotions and blow them up out of proportion, leaving us feeling very unhappy and disillusioned with the way that our lives are working. We tend to find ourselves feeling terrible about things that we do not need to feel terrible for. This can lead to a vicious cycle of guilt and anger toward ourselves that can be very difficult for us to get out of. We need some kind of interruption in order to help us to understand that we are in a negative mindset and we should begin to do our best to walk away from that kind of thinking.

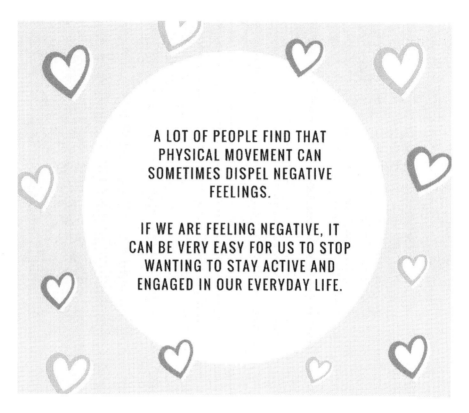

A LOT OF PEOPLE FIND THAT PHYSICAL MOVEMENT CAN SOMETIMES DISPEL NEGATIVE FEELINGS.

IF WE ARE FEELING NEGATIVE, IT CAN BE VERY EASY FOR US TO STOP WANTING TO STAY ACTIVE AND ENGAGED IN OUR EVERYDAY LIFE.

Another good way to help deal with the negative emotions is by learning some relaxation techniques. **These can help us to clear our minds and gain a new perspective on the negative events that are bothering us. We have to allow ourselves to be reasonable and try and put ourselves into another person's shoes,** especially if another person is being the source of our negativity. The better that we understand a situation, the easier it will be for us to acknowledge that we do not have to have a negative mindset about it. The more we learn about another person's perspective, the better we are able to cope with it from our own perspective. It can also make it easier for us to start implementing compromise that can be invaluable to maintaining healthy relationships and helping us to dispel negative feelings.

We can also educate ourselves about how emotions work.

Sometimes we are affected by things in our past that we don't even understand. They come up during the present and can sometimes make us disproportionately angry. A lot of people take out this kind of negativity on other people and it seems to feel extreme and unwarranted, even if the person who is angry feels like it is justified. Even if the anger is justified, sometimes is blown out of proportion because of emotions that we can't process, so they can be hard to understand.

The more we learn about our own traumatic incidences from the past and how the body works when we are confronted with whatever kinds of anger and loss that we have dealt with in the past, the more readily and easily we will be able to deal with negative emotions and dispel them in a healthy way that can allow us to maintain good ties with the people in our lives and have a healthier and happier relationship with our own inner selves as well.

A lot of people find that physical movement can sometimes dispel negative feelings. If we are feeling negative, it can be very easy for us to stop wanting to stay active and engaged in our everyday life. This is why many people who suffer from depression are also found sleeping in and having no motivation to go outside or exercise. Unfortunately, this lack of exercise can actually compound many negative emotions. Exercise and movement is a great way for us to start getting rid of negative energies. Many people find that when they are angry, they go into a state where they want to exercise or clean. This is actually a very healthy and positive thing for you to do and a great way for you to begin to deconstruct your negative emotions so that they no longer affect your life and harm your relationships.

Exercise has been physically proven to help us to reduce stress and anxiety, which are often triggers of great emotional distress. These types of negative emotions can be extremely harmful for us, and if we aren't able to deal with them properly then we find ourselves dealing with an extremely difficult situation. If we don't know how to relax, then we ultimately tend to pile on even more anxiety that can cause negativity to dwell deep within us. Relaxation can be extremely helpful when you are trying to change your life and think more positively. Positive thinking doesn't happen very easily if you are stressed out and anxious.

Anxiety can sometimes hijack our brains and causes a lot of discomfort. If we are able to begin to eliminate anxiety at the source, then we are taking a great step toward eliminating negative thoughts and negativity from our minds so that we can change our lives.

Dealing with our negativity is one of the most important aspects of learning how to think positively. If this is very difficult for you, and don't be surprised if it is, there are other sources that can help you. There are many counseling agencies and other free resources that can help you to deal with your negative emotions in a healthier way. You should check out a community health center for a better grasp on the local resources that are available to you.

Chapter 3: Staying Healthy and the Physical Benefits of Positive Thinking

Most of us know that there are health benefits to thinking positively, which is probably why you are reading this book. In order to understand these benefits in-depth, an entire chapter has been devoted to how positive thinking can improve your life and set you on a path of healing and longevity today.

Over the course of time, scientists have discovered that positive thinking can increase our lifespan. That is something that most people thrive to achieve, and something that can be accomplished with a lot more ease than most of us might believe. Optimism can help us to avoid pessimism and overall improve our level of satisfaction in life. The enhancement of our mood can help us to relieve stress and improve our autoimmune system. When people who had a positive and optimistic mindset were compared to people in a study who had a pessimistic mindset, the research concluded that those who were feeling more positive tend to have a longer lifespan than those who were pessimistic.

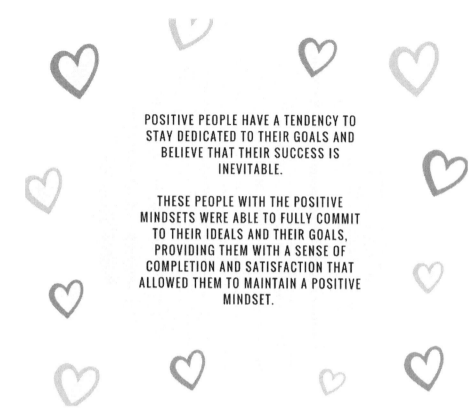

POSITIVE PEOPLE HAVE A TENDENCY TO STAY DEDICATED TO THEIR GOALS AND BELIEVE THAT THEIR SUCCESS IS INEVITABLE.

THESE PEOPLE WITH THE POSITIVE MINDSETS WERE ABLE TO FULLY COMMIT TO THEIR IDEALS AND THEIR GOALS, PROVIDING THEM WITH A SENSE OF COMPLETION AND SATISFACTION THAT ALLOWED THEM TO MAINTAIN A POSITIVE MINDSET.

Positive people have a tendency to stay dedicated to their goals and believe that their success is inevitable. These people with the positive mindsets were able to fully commit to their ideals and their goals, providing them with a sense of completion and satisfaction that allowed them to maintain a positive mindset. Without optimism and the belief that we are going to be able to accomplish anything in life, we become stressed out and defeated, and give up on ourselves before we even begin. We are never able to discover what we are fully capable of, and our potential is never completely realized. This is mentally draining and very difficult for us, and can cause many psychological and mental health problems that can even turn into physical ailments.

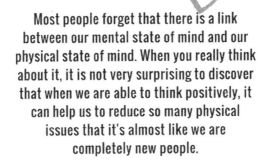

Most people forget that there is a link between our mental state of mind and our physical state of mind. When you really think about it, it is not very surprising to discover that when we are able to think positively, it can help us to reduce so many physical issues that it's almost like we are completely new people.

Positive thinking is one of the healthiest ways that we can begin to approach and deal with stress and depression, or other tragedies that are common in the life of a general human being.

Along with the stresses of physical ailments, there are problems that can plague us as we grow older. Fortunately, studies have shown that people who have a positive mindset are a lot less likely to have such a high rate of decline in our normal functions. As we age, our faculties tend to slow down or shut down completely, and the more negative our mindsets are, the more difficult it can be for our bodies to keep up maintenance that can be extremely important when it comes to performing daily and keeping us healthy longer.

Most of us simply acknowledge and accept the fact that when we age, it is kind of an opportunity for our bodies to collapse in on themselves and give up on life. However, once you are actually at that age, you are probably going to realize that you don't feel any different than you did at 20 years old. The only difference is physical, and if you need to change your mental state of thinking in order to keep your body healthier for longer, you might as well do so.

Studies have proven that it works, so if you want to be one of the 80% of people who feels a lot happier and a lot more functional as an elderly person, you are going to want to begin to start relishing in the benefits of positive thinking today. Mental and physical decline is not inevitable, and with a positive thinking mindset and regular exercise routines, you will be able to slow the signs of aging and avoid the deterioration that is often associated with it as well.

High sources of stress have been known to lead to many health problems and complications that can arise and cause us to feel a lot more unhealthy. Stress can seriously compromise our immune system and decrease our ability to fight off diseases. If we are unable to fight off disease, that means that we are going to be a lot more vulnerable as we age to issues that can bring us bodily harm. Most of us would like to avoid these types of health issues as much as possible. Fortunately, people who are able to convert their lives into thinking more positively are able to reduce the stress and anxiety that causes complications in our health that open us up to a wide range of medical problems.

You have probably seen on television or elsewhere that somebody with high cholesterol is supposed to avoid stress. If you couldn't figure out why, the trick is to understand cardiology. Cardiology is the study of the heart, and when our bodies are experiencing higher than normal amounts of cholesterol intake, this unhealthy aspect of our diet can cause complications. Fortunately, the simple act of thinking positively can help us to lower our cholesterol and avoid complications that arise when we are at risk of heart disease. Middle-aged people who participated in a study about optimism were discovered to have higher levels of bad cholesterol the more pessimistic they were. **This can be related to many things, such as poor diet and lack of exercise that is associated with a negative mindset,** but regardless, all of this is connected and the simple power of positive thinking can help us to lower our cholesterol, decrease stress, and soothe the risk of heart disease that we may experience.

Speaking of heart disease, cardiovascular disease is extremely lethal in North America. Optimism has been known to increase our ability to fight off cardiovascular diseases. Optimistic people have a much lower tendency toward heart disease than pessimistic people have. It's a huge percentage of a difference, coming in at a striking 73% lower chance of heart failure than those who are pessimistic thinkers. And really, this makes a lot of sense. People who suffer from stress often complain of chest pain. Just thinking negatively can cause the chest muscles to constrict and make our heart work overtime. These types of stresses are extremely unhealthy, and they are only impacted by the dangers of negative thinking. If you are able to begin to implement a positive thinking aspect into your life, you are going to have a much higher chance of staying healthier for longer and avoiding cardiovascular diseases that can end up being lethal.

Not only this, but we also find ourselves with a heightened ability to combat the common cold. A study has proven that people who have an optimistic mindset rather than a pessimistic mindset were much better able to mobilize their immune cells and allow themselves to fight off illnesses. This physical boost in the immune system is brought on by a lack of stress and an increase in cell-mediated immunity. Our cells stay healthier, the happier we are and the more positively we think. Without positive thinking in our lives, our cells tend to divide and have a much harder time working together to keep us safe and healthy.

We will have to take our bodies into our own hands, and begin to encourage ourselves to participate in a healthier lifestyle. Exercise has also been inextricably linked to longevity and a positive mindset. Exercise helps us to release energy and endorphins that make us feel great and encourage us to move forward on a path of positivity. Along with exercise comes the added benefit of helping our bodies to stay healthy and strong, giving us the chemical and physical boost we may need in order to stay focused on a positive mindset over a negative one. Many people have found benefits from yoga, and these types of exercises have been able to seriously reduce the risk of high cholesterol in middle-aged people.

Most people forget that there is a link between our mental state of mind and our physical state of mind. When you really think about it, it is not very surprising to discover that when we are able to think positively, it can help us to reduce so many physical issues that it's almost like we are completely new people. Positive thinking is one of the healthiest ways that we can begin to approach and deal with stress and depression, or other tragedies that are common in the life of a general human being.

This is especially important to consider when you are dealing with a teenager, as they go through many hormonal changes and imbalances that can cause them to feel physical mental and emotional stress. Teenagers who are able to turn to a more optimistic state of mind tend to have much lower rates of depression, turning to substance abuse, or other dangerous behavior.

All in all, the mental and physical aspects of positive thinking amounts to creating a great plethora of benefits for our health and well-being. If we are able to convert from negative thinking to positive thinking, and the chances are high that we will, we'll be able to cash in on the benefits that it can provide for our health and longevity as well as for our mental attitude.

Every one of us has struggles from time to time, but if we are suffering physically, thinking positively can help us to change that and it can help us to avoid feeling more negatively in the future.

Chapter 4: Stress and Anxiety

A lot of people find it difficult to remember that stress and anxiety is a very real problem that affects many people all over the world. It affects us physically as well as mentally and emotionally. If we have an overwhelming amount of stress and anxiety, these can create a lot of tension in the body. Stress can physically poison the bloodstream and cause a lot of health problems that can often be misdiagnosed and ultimately treated the wrong way.

A distinct disadvantage comes with the mistreatment of dangerous problems with chemical drugs that ultimately cause more side effects and issues to pile onto the original cause of the disorder. **The underlying cause continues to go untreated,** and your symptoms can just become exacerbated by the medication or further exposure to the cause of your stress and anxiety.

This can be dangerous for more than one reason. People who have high bouts of stress and anxiety are often looking for a cure. Many times, they look in the wrong place for that and wind up in a terrible cycle of narcotics abuse or other forms of self-medication that do not work and actually harm you. Some people begin to withdraw and become more afraid of social interactions. Sometimes you may find yourself distracting yourself with television and movies or other forms of media so that you do not have to deal with your feelings on a day-to-day basis, because they are unpleasant and difficult to understand. Going through stress can be extremely dangerous for us, both physically and mentally, and if we are high strung, this pollution of the body can make us more vulnerable to diseases and prevent new cells from forming that can help us to fight off harmful invaders in the body.

Stress can physically affect us in many ways. We can have frequent headaches, a hard time with swallowing or with keeping our mouth wet. It can cause us to feel dizzy and bring our heart rates very high. It can cause a lot of problems in our relationships because many times we feel very irritable and nervous. Sometimes we have breathing problems or we tend to sweat and twitch a lot more than is typically considered normal. Sometimes we are full of aches and pains that we don't know how we got.

Other times, it can make it difficult for us to learn things or focus on schoolwork or other important tasks in our daily lives because it seriously affects our ability to concentrate. There is too much energy in the blood that is not released physically and it can cause hormones to be released into the body that can begin to seriously harm us in a physical way.

This is particularly dangerous because it can suppress our immune system and lead to a whole slew of different diseases. If our immune system is not functioning well enough, that leaves us vulnerable to just about any bacteria that we come into contact with, even if on a normal day we would be feeling great and unaffected by those germs. It can cause many digestive disorders, including uncomfortable bouts of gastrointestinal problems.

This is because stress and anxiety are closely tied to our physical bodies, and when we feel nervous, we tend to feel nauseated or strange in the stomach. This is a physical response to stress and it can lead to even more difficulties in your digestive tract in the future.

Stress and anxiety has even been connected to a lot of dangerous issues with our muscles and our hearts. Many people who suffer from stress and hypertension for a long time tend to develop diseases in their hearts and suffer from heart attacks. This can be lethal and can cause extremely uncomfortable physical pain. Muscle tension is nothing to scoff at either, and this physical results of stress and anxiety is also dangerous and uncomfortable. It's another thing that can lead to headaches and other physiological issues.

Many people who have suffered from extreme bouts of stress and anxiety may find themselves dealing with intense bouts of short-term memory loss. While they may be able to understand and remember things that have happened in the past or over a course of time, extreme memory loss is common among many people who have suffered from traumatic and highly stressful events. Even if you have not suffered from trauma necessarily, if you are somebody who has a highly prone disposition to stress and anxiety, you may find yourself forgetting things short-term, such as where you put your glasses or if you bought coffee or not. This type of memory loss can be extremely disruptive to your everyday routine, so if you can find a way to cope with it, that is the best thing that you can do for yourself and your body at any given time.

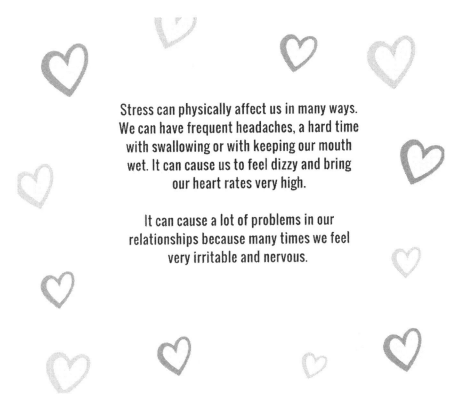

Stress can physically affect us in many ways.
We can have frequent headaches, a hard time
with swallowing or with keeping our mouth
wet. It can cause us to feel dizzy and bring
our heart rates very high.

It can cause a lot of problems in our
relationships because many times we feel
very irritable and nervous.

Many people have a hard time coping with stress and anxiety, because the way that the modern world is structured is not particularly encourage us to thrive and relax. If we are stressed out and panicking over little things, it may actually be because we have some kind of a stress or anxiety disorder that causes us a lot of difficulty in functioning in our day-to-day lives. A lot of people have a difficult time focusing their attention on pursuits that may leave them feeling more fulfilled and rewarded after a hard day of work.

People work hard so that they can continue to survive in today's society, but it does not leave a whole lot of time for you to get the things done that you feel will bring you the most joy and satisfaction. This can leave us feeling afraid for our own security if we decide to try and pursue more endeavors toward the things that we enjoy the most, and it can cause difficulties in our close and interpersonal relationships with other people because we are not able to fully immerse ourselves in the things that matter to us. This can make us extremely unhappy and irritable, causing a lot of negative tensions to arise between close family members and friends.

When something is hard to understand and to deal with is when we become consumed by stress and anxiety. When this happens, our brains are physically affected and it can sometimes cause us to act out irrationally and make connections that should not be made. For example, we may believe that something is our fault because we were simply there, we are a failure in life for making one mistake, or we may think that if we do not do something right on time, it will be the end of the world. These habits and negative ways of thinking can actually be very dangerous and disrupt our inner peace. Fortunately, there is a solution that many people have overlooked over the years, but it has started to get the attention that it deserves. The solution is positive thinking.

Chapter 5 – Circling Thoughts

Circling thoughts is a term that is used to describe the thoughts that plague our minds that we do not want. It is kind of an obsessive-compulsive thing that our brain does that brings us around and around to the negative ways of thinking that we are trying to eliminate in order to thrive in a new life full of positive thinking. Circling thoughts can make this impossible, because we have gotten into the habit so frequently of allowing these thoughts to run rampant in our minds and take on a lot of importance and meaning that they should not have. Fortunately for us, there are ways that we can work through circling thoughts so that they do not become so all-encompassing in our minds.

Circling thoughts generally abound as a result of unwanted stress and anxiety. People who have obsessive-compulsive disorder may be very familiar with the ideas of circling thoughts. **Obsessive-compulsive disorder** is actually an anxiety disorder, that has been set upon and triggered by trauma or other events that make a person vulnerable to the whims of their anxieties and their brains. Fortunately, circling thoughts have been identified and are able to be interrupted and intercepted. These thoughts are often scary and dark, or negative and difficult for people to stop thinking about. It's a very negative aspect of dealing with a stress and anxiety associated problem, and whether we have a disorder or not, these unwanted circling thoughts can start to take control of our lives and leave us feeling very powerless to take control.

If you are suffering or have ever suffered from circling thoughts, take comfort in the fact that many other people have experienced this problem as well. We can deal with this in a healthy and constructive way though, so don't feel even more anxiety knowing that your anxiety causes these problems. One of the best things that we can do for circling thoughts is to interrupt them and stop them in their tracks. This may seem impossible at first, but it is actually one of the most proven methods possible to stop the circling thoughts in your mind so that you are able to fully concentrate all of your mind power on positive thinking and improving your life.

Circling thoughts are dangerous because they are like a spiral that goes down the drain. We do not end up seeing the light of day again if we allow ourselves to get stuck in a circling thought that is plaguing us. Those of us who have been haunted by circling thoughts know that they are sometimes very unpleasant, and they can make us worry about things that ultimately turn out to be just fine. Circling thoughts are often the result of worry, and something that you should try to keep in mind about worrying is that you can't control every single situation that you find yourself in. All you can do is identify the areas where you can take control and make changes.

Otherwise, if you do not have control, you are going to have to make peace with that fact and allow yourself to accept that it is out of your hands and there is nothing more that you can do about it. Believe it or not, this will provide you with an immense sense of peace and closure, because you have done your best and you have done everything that you can to control the situation. Now all you can do is control how you feel about the inevitable results.

Circling thoughts are scary because we don't always know what to do about them. Most people give them extra attention because sometimes they are so bizarre and out of the ordinary that they make us feel uncomfortable or disturbed.

However, putting too much emphasis on your circling thoughts actually just blows them up out of proportion and gives them more power over you and your mindset. Instead of trying to take apart your circling thought, acknowledge that many times it is irrational and that you are taking the steps you need to take in order to deal with whatever issue you are thinking about.

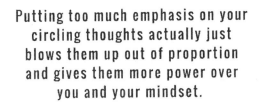

Putting too much emphasis on your circling thoughts actually just blows them up out of proportion and gives them more power over you and your mindset.

Instead of trying to take apart your circling thought, acknowledge that many times it is irrational and that you are taking the steps you need to take in order to deal with whatever issue you are thinking about.

Once you have acknowledged this, push it to the back of your mind and don't give it any more attention at all. You should try to make the choice not to encourage your own negative thought patterns, even if this means that you have to keep a journal in which you begin to keep track of the thoughts that you are having so that you know which ones are unhealthy and circling, and what to do when you are dealing with them. Interrupt them as much as possible.

Stress and anxiety are definitely caused by imbalances in our lives, and you should never feel as if you are damaged or broken because you are suffering from stress and anxiety. Stress and anxiety are actually reactions that most people have to difficult and stressful situations that put our bodies out of balance. This is generally a very common thing to deal with, and people who are able to stay in balance do so by understanding that it is natural to have thoughts that you do not want, and if you don't want them there you don't have to pay attention to them. All you can really do is begin to think about something better or consider what you are doing that can start to soothe these thoughts and lay them to rest.

One example of something that you can do is to interrupt the thoughts by finding some kind of affirmation or mantra that will help you to focus on the positive aspects of your life or to simply distract you from the negative thoughts. If the negative thoughts are too consuming and you are not able to deconstruct them in a healthy way, to the point that you are suffering from stress and anxiety, you need to try to remap your neural pathways so that they will connect to better things, rather than continuing to connect to patterns that continue to make us miserable.

Sometimes, when we are having an anxiety attack due to circling thoughts, it might be best for you to begin thinking about what your body is doing physically. **This is called mindfulness, and if you are able to focus on the here**

and now, the strange and panicking sensations that you may feel during an episode of a panic attack can begin to decrease and you will begin to feel a lot more in control of your situation and surroundings.

You have to be your own biggest supporter in this case, because many people are not going to be able to understand what you're going through. You can talk yourself through anything, and prepare a speech that you know and understand for any time that you are having a panic attack or any other type of anxiety issue. You can use all of the tips in the second part of this book to help you to move forward and dealing with your anxiety and stress so that you can begin to focus on the solutions that positive thinking can give to you. Replacing your anxious thoughts with positive thoughts is one of the only ways that you can combat unwanted circling thoughts that arise from anxiety and other negative problems such as stress.

Positive thinking is extremely powerful, so if you are able to stop thinking of things in a very doomed mentality, such as thinking to yourself that it is impossible for you to achieve something, you can begin to rephrase the way that you are thinking in order to combat this unwanted and circling thought in your mind.

Instead of saying "I can never do this," say instead, "I can do this if..." and see the difference starting to take place in your life immediately. If you are having a circling thought that will not go away and it is one of a worry, **remind yourself that you have done the best you can and the results are out of your hands**. And then begin to think about something more positive that you do have control over. This will help to ground you and give you more control and power over your mindset so that you can began to veer toward a path of positive thinking no matter what difficulties you are going through.

37

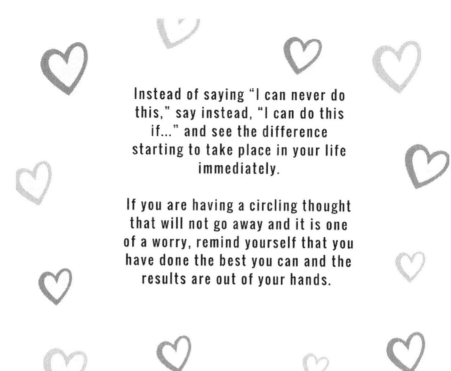

Instead of saying "I can never do this," say instead, "I can do this if..." and see the difference starting to take place in your life immediately.

If you are having a circling thought that will not go away and it is one of a worry, remind yourself that you have done the best you can and the results are out of your hands.

Part Two: How To Become A Positive Thinker

Chapter 6 – Habits of the Positive Person

Positive thinking comes more easily for some than for others, and the people who have discovered the powers of positive thinking all share some similar habits. In the second section, we are going to cover all of the different ways that we can become a positive thinker, and delve into the details about the habits that most people who are positive thinkers can share.

If you try thinking positively for yourself, it may be easy to speculate that it couldn't possibly work. Fortunately, you couldn't be more wrong. Positive thinking is one of the most beneficial strategies for interrupting physical and mental problems. It has even been used in order to help us to combat cancer, as it reinforces our cells and begins to improve our immune systems when everything else seems like it's going to fail.

All of us deserve an opportunity to think positively and enjoy and experience our lives in a way that brings us more benefits than consequences.

Negative thinking can impact us on every level, so it is important to educate ourselves on the habits of positive people. If you have a harder time staying positive, observing people who stay positive can be very helpful. You will come to find out that the habits of positive people are very healthy and allow them to stay happier for longer than if they were doing the same things that a negative person was doing.

For example, **many positive people tend to get a lot of exercise.** This helps our bodies to physically become stronger and healthier, reinforcing all of the chemicals and processes that our bodies need in order to thrive and flourish and grow. Without exercise, we are left to our own devices and have a much more difficult time dealing with anxiety and stress.

All the energy goes nowhere, and it comes out in bad ways, sometimes even in the form of panic attacks or other episodes that can leave us embarrassed or angry. This can severely damage our relationships as well as preventing us from having a happy or sound state of mind.

Positive people also tend to know who to trust and who their friends should be. They don't tolerate anybody giving them too much flack, and they can identify and avoid sources of toxic emotions quickly and easily. They remove the people from their lives who do not help them to feel good, and do everything they can in order to maintain healthy relationships with their friends and family members. Positive people have a tendency to feel in control and assume that they might as well try to achieve their goals because otherwise they may never happen.

If you have a strong aversion to success, then you are going to stay unhappy. Most people with a negative thinking pattern tend to want to avoid success, for one psychological reason or another. The positive people do not sabotage their own success, but rather encourage it and promote everything to fall in place as they want or need it to do.

The difference between positive people and negative people is how they think and nothing else.

It doesn't matter how many things you have or how much better off you are materially, or even where you live. It has very little to do with the physical, and everything to do with the mental. **A person with nothing can very easily be much happier and more positive than a person who thinks they have everything.** Of course there are physical habits that can help you to overcome negativity and feel more positive on the whole, and these will be explored later in the section.

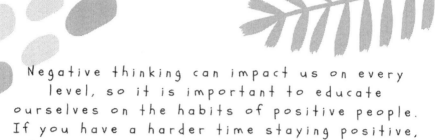

Negative thinking can impact us on every level, so it is important to educate ourselves on the habits of positive people. If you have a harder time staying positive, observing people who stay positive can be very helpful. You will come to find out that the habits of positive people are very healthy and allow them to stay happier for longer than if they were doing the same things that a negative person was doing.

Chapter 7 – How Do You Talk To Yourself?

We would probably be surprised if anybody spoke to us the way we speak to ourselves. Most of us are very negative and hard on ourselves, **and if we were ever able to really look at the impact our words have on our state of mind by imagining that other people were saying this to us, we would realize that most of the time we are really big bullies to ourselves.**

If you are able to take a tape recorder and speak out loud the thoughts that you have, you would probably realize just how negative you are and how harshly this can impact you on a day-to-day basis. Nobody deserves to be spoken to in such a cruel way, and so it is extremely important for you to be able to speak to yourself kindly and respectfully whether you feel that it is important or not.

If we were ever able to really look at the impact our words have on our state of mind by imagining that other people were saying this to us, we would realize that most of the time we are really big bullies to ourselves.

Most of us begin to talk to ourselves the way we are used to being spoken to, or the way that we expect to be spoken to. We hold ourselves to a very high standard and this can really get in the way of our ability to feel positive and think positively. If we become extremely negative and allow this to damage us and the ways that any bullying would do, then it is very easy to understand why we might feel very defeated and anxious and depressed.

If we are not on our own side, then who in the world will be? If we feel so badly about ourselves that we have to constantly keep our inner dialogue on critique rather than on support, then the negativity that we are unleashing in our own lives can be poisonous and lethal.

Much of the time we believe that we are worse than we really are, and we often skew the way that we think of ourselves and our accomplishments or our goals. We tend to be very negative and defeating, talking ourselves out of taking risks and seeking opportunities to improve ourselves or move forward in projects that are very meaningful for us. Some of this is not negative, and can actually help us to accomplish things that may be difficult otherwise. However, adding commentary that is not objective when we fail or succeed can provide us with a fragile sense of self that feels inadequate and struggles to find the positive light in many situations.

Most of us are very used to bullying ourselves and we don't generally see any reason why we should change the way that we think or speak to ourselves within our own mind. But what we don't realize is that our negativity is often very exaggerated and it can consume us entirely very quickly and easily.
Our perception is always skewed by biases and pre-existing opinions about the world and the way that we think people are or should be.

One of the biggest and most dangerous problems with self-talk is that we assume that we are the ultimate authority. We are not usually able to call ourselves out on flawed ways of thinking, and we assume that we are constantly right about the inner voice that is inside of us all. It comes out as we are trying to understand new situations and feelings, and it can sometimes lead us to a very bad place if we are not objective or reasonable with ourselves.

If we do not give ourselves the same forgiveness that we tend to give to other people, this can leave us feeling extremely terrible even if we cannot pinpoint the exact reason why. It's important to be able to challenge yourself and understand that not everything you believe about yourself is true. Imagine telling a friend or a family member who loves you more than life itself how you think about yourself and your failures or accomplishments. They will probably look at you as if you are crazy and tell you to be nicer to yourself.

Most of us are very used to bullying ourselves and we don't generally see any reason why we should change the way that we think or speak to ourselves within our own mind. But what we don't realize is that our negativity is often very exaggerated and it can consume us entirely very quickly and easily. Our perception is always skewed by biases and pre-existing opinions about the world and the way that we think people are or should be.

Even if we are generally reasonable people, negativity and self-loathing can show up in many different ways and lead to a lot of problems down the road, especially when it comes to blocking our ability to think positively. Many of us feel angry or depressed at times, and most of us feel anxious. If we are able to identify these feelings within ourselves as they are happening, we can begin to examine what it is on our mind that is making us feel this way. If we can do this, we can begin to compartmentalize our emotions. This way, we can begin to deconstruct the way that we think so that it can become more positive rather than negative over the course of time.

You're going to have to be extra honest with yourself about your negativity and the way that you think. You can't convince your negative thoughts and the unwanted circling thoughts that can sometimes arise and we are feeling emotional. We have to try and remember that negativity can sometimes stop the blood in our brains from flowing so that we are unable to fully grasp the gravity of the situation. This can make us act out and cause us unnecessary grief. It can lead us to harm ourselves and a damper in the relationships that we care the most about. If we do not understand the cues that lead us to needing to get some introspection, we may not be able to reflect well enough on our negative self-talk to challenge it and change the way that we think.

Positive thinking can cause us to begin to feel better about ourselves than we ever did before. If we stop thinking that we are such terrible people, or so ugly, or so incompetent, then we are going to begin to believe that we have everything that it takes to make it in our lives and succeed in our goals. The only chance that we have of achieving our dreams is to take a risk, and most people who are consumed with negative self-talk do not find the risk to be worth it. **They feel defeated before they begin and don't even want to start on a new project.** This is extremely discouraging and can cause you to feel extremely depressed. If we are not going after what we want, then we begin to feel as if nothing in the world is worth it.

Sometimes we may even begin to question our worth or the worth of our existence if we are not able to move forward on the projects that we care the most about. This is when anxiety and depression can become very dangerous, and self-talk can really disrupt your sense of safety and security. Many people who suffer from depression and anxiety have very skewed ways of thinking and they are not able to accurately perceive the situations around them. They misread things and blame themselves for things that are not their fault.

If you find yourself doing this, you're going to have to keep in mind actively throughout the day that you might be wrong. **In fact, the chances are high that you are wrong.**

People are not always going to be out to get you. People are not always going to wonder what is wrong with you for simply being yourself. There is a lot about you that is wonderful and good, and there are a lot of thoughts that you have that are reasonable and healthy. You should focus on these instead of focusing on the negative self-talk that makes you bully yourself too much.

If you have a problem with negative self-talk, there are ways you can help this. First of all, you can begin to gauge **reality versus your perception**. You're going to need concrete evidence, and a way to measure yourself up against the facts. First of all, you're going to have to figure out what it is that makes you believe what you do. You're going to have to see both sides of it. Why do you think what you do, what is your evidence for this, and what could possibly dispute the way that you think? You're going to have to ask yourself whether or not you are jumping to conclusions that are **too rash and too negative**. You'll have to do some research, even if that means asking people their true and honest opinions so that you can hold onto them during times of crisis.

You're also going to have to understand that there are many other possibilities out there. Your explanation for what is going on is not always going to be the correct explanation. It could mean other things, and it could be completely different than what you think it is. If you are constantly thinking negatively, you're going to have to remind yourself that there are other **ways to view the situation in a more positive light**. If you find this difficult, catch yourself during a negative moment and wonder how somebody positive might be thinking about the same situation that you are putting yourself. This can often help us to put things into perspective. Perspective is something that we have a difficult time with, especially if we are suffering with stress and anxiety and negative thinking patterns.

We have to begin to be conscious of the fact that we are being negative so that we can combat these negative thoughts with positive possibilities. For example, if you are feeling like you are in a crisis and it is feeling very negative, you're going to have to be realistic with yourself. **Is what you are worried about going to matter in the future? Will it even matter in five minutes? Even if it does matter, what is the worst thing that you could expect to happen in the situation and how likely is it that this negative event is going to affect you? It's pretty unlikely isn't it?** The worst case scenario is a very low statistic probability. Instead of thinking about the worst that could happen, think about what the best thing to happen will be. Instead of dreading the worst, instead, hope for the best.

In every cloud, you have to seek the silver lining and do your best to figure out if there is anything that you can take away of value from the situation that you are in.

Is what you are worried about going to matter in the future? Will it even matter in five minutes? Even if it does matter, what is the worst thing that you could expect to happen in the situation and how likely is it that this negative event is going to affect you?

It's pretty unlikely isn't it?

Next you have to be proactive. Each of us have goals and hopes and dreams that we would like to accomplish in the near future. If we are constantly in crisis and unable to think rationally or believe in our goals, it is going to be extremely difficult for us to accomplish anything. If we are always so convinced that we shouldn't even began, or we are worthless before we start, or there is no hope in success, then we will never be able to move forward in the things that we are truly passionate about.

The rut that we find ourselves in will be deep and we will be stuck there for a long time. Instead, we should think about our goals, and decide whether or not the way that we are thinking, whether that is negative or positive, will help us to achieve what we want to accomplish in the world. We have to determine whether or not the way we are thinking is **going to be constructive** when we are attempting to solve problems. We are also going to have to figure out if we can

take anything of value away from our situation and find out
if we can use any of our experience as a learning experience
so that we can do better in the future.

**Interrupting a negative thought processes is
extremely important.** If we talk to ourselves in a way that
would make us cringe if we heard someone else talking to us
that way, or somebody else being spoken to that way, that's a
sure sign that we need to start identifying these negative self-
speech patterns and nip them in the bud.

**Everybody deserves to feel safe and secure, even in
their own minds. The more negative you are to
yourself, the harder it is going to be for you to
succeed in the future.**

Everybody deserves the opportunity to feel great about their
lives and the possibilities that they have open to them at any
given moment. If you are too busy talking down to yourself
and making yourself feel inadequate, then it is time to start
calling yourself out on these negative voices in your head
so that you can begin to take the steps that you need to
change your life and implement positive thinking.

Chapter 8 – Physical and Mental Benefits of Humor

It's no mistake that many people believe that laughter is the best medicine. Laughter is extremely powerful, and it has the ability to help us to find relief in almost any given situation. Most of us are able to laugh frequently throughout the day, and this can cause us to feel a lot better about everything that we have experienced or continue to experience. It is an extremely amazing function that our bodies do naturally to help us relieve stress, stop feeling acute repercussions of pain, and to ease the spikes of conflict and confrontation. It can help us to restore our energy and heal from tremendous bouts of stress and difficulty. It can help us to improve the immune system and avoid diseases. Not only that, but it is one of the **healthiest and fastest ways** for us to change from a negative mindset to a positive mindset instantly.

In the blink of an eye, something can cause us to laugh and release endorphins in our bodies. This release of endorphins can help us to feel empowered and stronger, at the same time allowing us to relax and take away the tension and the pain of stress. After a good laugh, our muscles feel a lot more at ease, which is extremely beneficial if you are generally used to living in a mindset full of anxiety and stress, or constantly living in a negative frame of mind. **If you thought badly of yourself**, nothing can help you to ease those thoughts more than laughing at your own negative thinking. Interrupt these thoughts by saying how silly you are for thinking that you are so much worse than you actually are. You will begin to feel better in no time, and understand that you are telling yourself the truth.

The stress hormones that are released into our bodies will eventually diminish the more we laugh. Laughter can also help us to prevent heart disease, which is another dangerous side effect of having too much stress and anxiety. Not only will these physical benefits be beneficial to people who have become used to living in a negative mindset, but it can also help us to strengthen our relationships and promote bonding between people who might otherwise have never given one another the time of day. Laughter is extremely helpful and can allow us to stop feeling tense and relieve the stress of any given situation. **It can leave us feeling great and happier than we have been in a long time.**

When it comes to the mental state of mind, it can actually help us to recharge and increase our energy levels. This can cause us to be able to focus a lot more easily, negating the short term memory loss that can be found with many stress and anxiety disorders and difficult moments. We can also begin to feel a lot less fearful and a lot more happy. It can allow us to stay strong in the face of tragedy and become an inspiration to other people who may need to hear and understand our positive point of view.

This can make us valuable in our social communities as well as resistant to any type of anxiety or negative emotion that can leave us reeling and wishing for relief. It can help us to change our perspective into a healthier one, and shift us from negative thinking to positive thinking in no time. We are able to be more objective and allow ourselves to fully appreciate all aspects of the situation. This way, negativity doesn't dwell within us and we are able to discharge whatever we are dealing with at the time.

If you don't know the way to make yourself laugh, just do your best to reach into your mind for something funny. Poke fun about something or play with something that is cute. You can watch funny television or movies, or listen to standup comedians.
You could enjoy other people's a sense of humor, or read funny books and learn jokes that can apply in any situation. It's always fun to goof around, and not only that but it is extremely beneficial. If you are able to integrate humor into your truest feelings, people will listen to your point of view without being quite as hurt or offended by it. **They will see your perspective and laugh at it, without feeling defensive.**

You will not feel defensive either, and it will allow you to practice being more spontaneous and uninhibited. This is the truest and most rewarding way to live, so if you are hoping for more ways to find humor in the world, surround yourself with things that are full of joy.

If you thought badly of yourself, nothing can help you to ease those thoughts more than laughing at your own negative thinking. Interrupt these thoughts by saying how silly you are for thinking that you are so much worse than you actually are.

You will begin to feel better in no time, and understand that you are telling yourself the truth.

Chapter 9 – Cutting Out Toxic People

One of the things that you can do in order to manage your stress levels and open your mind to positive thinking is to remove toxic people from your life. **Toxic people are the fastest way to high levels of stress that there is**. Their opinions are often negative and insulting, and they are able to bring you down at a moment's notice no matter how happy you may have been the moment before. Positive people will not put you down or encourage your negative way of thinking. They will help you to understand that you do have flaws in your negative thinking, and they will help you to balance them out and feel more joyful rather than more stressed out.

Dealing with toxic people is a lot like living with people who spit poison at you any chance they get. It's a very noxious environment that can infect you even if you don't realize that you are being affected. Nobody has the right to bring other people's mood down simply to alleviate or relieve their own negativity. Unfortunately, **this is exactly what toxic people do.** They don't stay open to more positive frames of mind, because it is more rewarding in their minds for them to be negative and to put others down.

You should never stick around somebody who is seeming to enjoy your misery, because if they are doing this that means they have deeper psychological issues then you need to deal with. A healthy person knows how to dispel the negativity properly, and it will not drag you down with them.

Toxic people in your life are people that you cannot possibly avoid, you are going to have to learn how to **set limits with them** so that they do not start to deplete you and set you into an area where you are thinking negatively as well. There is nothing more contagious the negativity, and toxic people are just brimming with it and itching to thoroughly at anybody who will take it. To begin to set limits of the toxic person, you can begin to distance yourself whenever you find yourself feeling a little bit compromised. You can show sympathy but you do not have to become completely engulfed in their drama or their pity parties.

Instead of allowing them to continue pulling you into their drama and their complaints, then you are going to have to talk about how they might be able to fix the problem rather than just complain about it. Most of the time, they do not really want to fix the problem, and they would actually prefer to complain and spread negativity whenever they can. If this is the case, you can just **tell them that you did your best to try and help them** but since they are not open to your solutions you have better things to do. If they are open to the idea of solving problems, then you can help them to come up with constructive solutions. **Otherwise, you can remove yourself from the situation at this point and stay healthy.**

In order to deal with toxic people, if you are forced to deal with them, you will have to stay in full control of your emotional state of being. If you begin to find yourself feeling overwhelmed and losing control of your perspective because their negativity is so difficult for you to handle, then you are going to have to maintain a good distance so that you do not become tainted by their negativity. People who are irrational and difficult to deal with should probably not be dealt with. Some people only want to be around chaotic situations, and if you are not helping them to create the chaos, they will try to create the chaos in you until you are part of it. You need to stay away from these kinds of problems and the people who encourage them.

Toxic people in your life are people that you cannot possibly avoid, you are going to have to learn how to set limits with them so that they do not start to deplete you and set you into an area where you are thinking negatively as well.

It's also helpful to remember that nobody can control how you feel about anything.

Although toxic people's desire to bring us down can be very stupid at times, you do not have to succumb to an emotional reaction to their stupidity. If you distance yourself far enough, you will end up being able to realize that most of the negativity is harming other people or themselves more than it has to harm you. You do not have to focus on the negativity that they are trying to spread. You do not have to let them change the way that you feel, or to cross the boundaries that you need to set for yourself.

You have to constantly maintain those boundaries so that they do not cross them and cause you to feel more compromised then you should be. You have to be consistent about your boundaries so that they begin to learn that they cannot cross them and you are not going to tolerate any of their nonsensical behavior. Eventually they will catch on that you are not part of the game and probably let you go, unless you are unable to continue maintaining your boundaries.

You have to always make sure that you are getting enough rest and you need to make sure that you are not always surrounded by people who are draining your energy instead of helping you to maintain high and productive positive energy levels. Avoid the negative and toxic people as much as you possibly can; that is the only way for you to truly make a difference when it comes to negative self-talk and negative emotions and thinking.

In order to deal with toxic people, if you are forced to deal with them, you will have to stay in full control of your emotional state of being.

If you begin to find yourself feeling overwhelmed and losing control of your perspective because their negativity is so difficult for you to handle, then you are going to have to maintain a good distance so that you do not become tainted by their negativity.

Anybody who is surrounded by negativity all the time will begin to get infected by it one way or another. Everybody is able to move forward in their lives if they can continue to see the possibilities around them and seize opportunities that will move them forward. Unfortunately, these opportunities become impossible to find if you are stuck in a negative mindset.

If the world always seems dangerous and cruel, as if it is working against you or some other person who is constantly bringing you down with their negativity and toxic attitude, then you are never going to be able to fully focus your mind on positive thinking.

You need to distance yourself as much as possible. The best case scenario is that you will remove these people from your life as much as you can, **however it is possible that this is not completely within your power,** so you will have to learn how to establish your boundaries and stay positive on your own. **The next couple of chapters will help you do this.**

Chapter 10 – Holding Yourself Accountable For How You Think

The last chapter was a great introduction to how important it is to hold yourself accountable for how you are thinking. We covered negative self-talk in a former chapter, but we didn't completely talk about how you can take steps to eliminate these terrible thoughts from your mind. One of the only ways that you can do this is to begin to hold yourself accountable for how you think. **If you are able to understand that the way you speak to yourself in your own mind is not positive or productive, you are taking the first step toward holding yourself accountable for how you think.**

This can be very difficult for many people, because the way we think is often very habitual. Fortunately, there are strategies to help you to understand why it is important to hold yourself accountable and to help you catch all of the negative emotions and feelings that circle in your mind on a constant basis. Most of us are pretty good at regulating our self-talk, but if we are dealing with a lot of stressful and negative situations then it can become out of hand. This is why it is important to manage these thoughts and learn how to see them from a new perspective. Holding ourselves accountable is the only way to help us do this.

First of all, it might help you to get a journal so that you can begin to recognize the negative thought patterns as they arise. When you begin to think about something negative, write down your negative thought and whatever might be associated with it. Wait for a while until you calm down and then go back and read about what you were thinking. You may often find that your thoughts were **exaggerated perceptions** about what was truly happening in reality. This can help you to recognize that this is a negative thought and that it is **disrupting your life** and state of mind. If you do not want to be plagued by this negative thought anymore, then you will have to actively try to remember that it is negative and to combat it with more positive thoughts in the future.

While you are still feeling happy and rational, instead of negative and unhappy, then you should try and look at your thought in a new light. **What is reality truly like here?** What are some possibilities that are happening that may cause your thought to be irrational? Even if what you are thinking is true, how could you see it in a better light? Is there a way to add humor to your perception so that it can diffuse the negativity and stop stewing in your mind and tainting your ability to think in a positive way? There are many times that our negative emotions are warranted, and it is okay to feel angry at times. When it is unhealthy though, it can be very difficult for us to separate ourselves from the irrational thoughts and they can become consuming and powerful burdens in our lives that can prevent us from moving forward.

Once we have begun to recognize the general patterns of negative thinking that we have constructed in our own minds, we are going to have to do our best to interrupt them before they begin changing our moods. If we can succeed in this, we can succeed in changing our negative thought patterns into positive ones before we are taking down a road that we do not want to go down. This is an extremely important step in changing our lives, so we should do it right. Even if you do not want to keep your journal, pay close attention to your thoughts and stay accountable to them. **Make sure you know what is rational and what is exaggerated, and find a way to diffuse the negativity associated with everything in your life.**

Write down your negative thought and whatever might be associated with it. Wait for a while until you calm down and then go back and read about what you were thinking.

You may often find that your thoughts were exaggerated perceptions about what was truly happening in reality. This can help you to recognize that this is a negative thought and that it is disrupting your life and state of mind.

If you do not want to be plagued by this negative thought anymore, then you will have to actively try to remember that it is negative and to combat it with more positive thoughts in the future.

Chapter 11 – Letting Go Of Control

Something that a lot of people struggle with, particularly in the context of today's society, is letting go of the fact that we do not have control over everybody or everything. This can cause us to feel anxious and irritable, especially when we are feeling worried about our future. Negative thoughts can abound very quickly when we find ourselves confronted with a situation where we feel like we have lost control. This can happen frequently, especially if we are parents or we are in a stressful work environment where everything can impact us negatively if it doesn't work out exactly how we hope it will.

Unfortunately, this type of stress is highly unhealthy, and if we are not able to understand and reconcile ourselves with the fact that we should always allow ourselves to let go of control to some extent, then we will find ourselves full of negativity and very likely to take it out on other people. Losing control is a difficult thing for most of us and we often begin to feel very unhappy with ourselves and the world around us. We start to lose control of our tempers, maybe by calling ourselves names and feeling inferior for not being able to hold on to things that may not have been possible to hold onto. **We take things personally that we**

shouldn't take personally, because we do not allow ourselves to look at the situation from all angles.

For example, if you have lost your job because somebody else was hired and their skill level is higher than yours, it is pretty likely that you should not be taking it personally. If they were taught at a different school or they know different things than you do, this is something objective **that was out of your control**. You did not have any say in whether or not the bosses met the person who is going to replace you. It is not because you are inferior that somebody else was taught a different skills set than you have. You have to try and stay objective and allow yourself to believe that sometimes losing control of a situation is not within your power to change. Some of us are able to maintain control to some degree, but only by alienating the good favor of others. We have to understand that there is a balance to try and achieve so that we are not constantly feeling stressed out and negative about the fact that we do not always have the power that we wish we did.

Sometimes during illness, letting go of control is one of the only things that can bring us peace. Whatever is meant to happen will happen in this case, and there is not much that we can do either way to change the outcome of certain problems. All we can do is our best, and even if we make the right decision for the meantime, sometimes that's not the right decision for the long term and vice versa. We can never fully know if we are going in the right direction or not, **and we can only try and have faith that the area that we are headed will be okay. We have done our best and that's the best we can ever do.**

It's obvious that having faith can be very difficult for many people, but allowing yourself to surrender to the fact that there is never going to be an opportunity for you to be 100% in control of every aspect of your life can provide you with a sense of peace that you may never have felt before. **All of us are constantly struggling to try and maintain a sense**

of security that is otherwise impossible in a world so full of variables.

If we can only allow ourselves to forgive ourselves for not having the control we wish we did, then we will be able to surrender a lot of our negative thinking and turn toward a positive state of mind instead. **Sometimes this is all you can do, and knowing this can bring you a great amount of peace.**

You have to try and stay objective and allow yourself to believe that sometimes losing control of a situation is not within your power to change.

Some of us are able to maintain control to some degree, but only by alienating the good favor of others.

We have to understand that there is a balance to try and achieve so that we are not constantly feeling stressed out and negative about the fact that we do not always have the power that we wish we did.

Chapter 12 – You Can't Change Others – Only Yourself

Thinking that it is okay to surrender control sometimes is especially true when we take into consideration the fact that you cannot change other people. You may believe that doing so is the only way that you will ever be able to find happiness and peace in your relationships, but the fact is that you will never be able to change somebody else or stop them from being who they are or thinking how they think. Even if the way they think is a constant source of stress and anxiety for us, other people are going to constantly have their own opinions and throw them around whenever they feel like it's necessary.

Nobody knows exactly what you are thinking except yourself, until you let other people in on it. Other people have begun to utilize this strategy in order to make themselves feel more important for to assert their power over a certain situation. Although this can be deplorable at times and it can severely ruin our chances of feeling positive at any given time, the fact remains that we are not always going to be able to change the way they think or feel, and they will gladly tell you so.

Although this can be very frustrating, it's important to remember that we are still able to change our perspective on the situations that we find ourselves in. Whether they're infuriating and frustrating or not, we do not have to stay personally attached to these negative feelings. If we can become objective and try and see every situation from other people's point of view, there is going to be a much easier transition between you thinking positively versus the way you were when you were thinking negatively. It can be very difficult for you to change your perspective and change yourself, and it can take a lifetime before you are feeling up to the challenge. Fortunately though, everybody who is anybody is able to control themselves to some extent, and the power that we wield over our own brains and perceptions is incredible.

The same is true of the past, if we really think about it. We can never change what has happened in our past, and we can never change what other people have done to us in the past or what they are doing to us in the present moment, unless they are particularly self-aware or you are able to defend yourself in a way that is healthy and nonexplosive for the both of you. **It's extremely dangerous for people to assume that they can change other people.** This is something that can often lead into abusive relationships that put somebody into a power dynamic with a toxic person who tries to put them down in order to raise themselves up.

If you believe that you can change somebody else and their negative thought patterns and behaviors, you are sorely mistaken. It is a very difficult thing just to consider the fact that you can change yourself, let alone the idea that maybe you can try to change someone else as well. Unfortunately, you can never change somebody who is not willing to change. You would have to be able to get them into some kind of mindset where they are open to the possibility that they are wrong, and gently guide them into the ways that they can begin to work on the things that are difficult for them.

However, the follow-through is very difficult and can be impossible for many people if they are not serious about changing their lives. The powers of positive thinking can help us to do this a lot more easily, but if you are with somebody who refuses to try to find the positivity in any situation, then you are defeated before you even begin.

You should never try and waste your energy on changing someone else. It will never work and you will just find yourself frustrated and confused about what you are doing wrong. Unfortunately, there is a lot that you are doing wrong if you believe that you have any power over how other people perceive the world.

You can give them little tips or advice, but you can never change them. The only person on earth you have the power to change is yourself.

If you believe that you can change
somebody else and their negative
thought patterns and behaviors, you
are sorely mistaken.

It is a very difficult thing just to
consider the fact that you can
change yourself, let alone the idea
that maybe you can try to change
someone else as well.
Unfortunately, you can never
change somebody who is not willing
to change.

You would have to be able to get
them into some kind of mindset
where they are open to the
possibility that they are wrong, and
gently guide them into the ways
that they can begin to work on the
things that are difficult for them.

Chapter 13 – How To Stop Worrying And Be Happier

Unfortunately, there is no miraculous cure for worry, but there is a way that we can begin to change our perspective on the things that cause us concern. Everybody is going to be bound to worry about something one way or another. Unfortunately, that is just the nature of life.

Things aren't always guaranteed, and everything that we hold close to us can easily be taken away. This can be very disturbing for people who have a hard time dealing with their emotions, and sometimes worry can turn into even more intense disorders like anxiety or other kinds of problems. A lot of worry can stem from anxiety as well, leading us to feel a lot more negative and stay plagued by very intense and misleading emotions that cause our perspective to be skewed by our negativity and fears.

When we are acting out of fear, it is very difficult for us to be sincere. All of us are extremely vulnerable to our own fears and worries, which can often bring us into a difficult situation. Worrying and anxiety can ultimately cause us to have many health problems, even if they do not seem to appear straightaway. Whether we see it or not, anxiety and worry can cause hypertension and other stress hormones to be released in the body that are extremely hazardous to our health. These hormones can actively harm us and compromise our immune systems, which can cause us to be physically ill more frequently, ironically lending more power to our negative thinking.

Most people with anxiety are trying too hard to stay in control of everything all at one time. Maybe people who suffer from anxiety have had things happen to them in the past where they were not able to stay in control and it caused them to watch their life as it slowly seems to fall apart right before their eyes. For this reason, staying in control seems very attractive as a possibility, and whether it is practical or not is another issue. When they can't, it can cause panic as it seems their lives are again heading in a terrible direction.

In some ways, we should try hard to get rid of our worries. In other ways though, there are things that can help us stay on track and achieve our responsibilities. If we have goals that we want to accomplish, if we are worried about losing track or losing side of these goals, then is actually a bad thing to relax and stop worrying about where our project is heading at any given time. However, sometimes it is not such a great thing for us to be worrying and it can deeply impact our state of mind, including our health and well-being. **In order to feel happier, we will have to start learning how to stop worrying so that we can allow ourselves to indulge in a positive state of mind rather than a negative one.**

One common source of worry and concern that prevents happiness is too much clutter. All of us tend to have a lot more material items than we need. These can often become a source of anxiety when our home becomes cluttered. If we want to reduce anxiety and worry, we should reduce the things that we have to worry about. We should get rid of whatever we don't use, or give away or put away things that may be sentimental but are not serving us in the here and now. Reducing the clutter in your life is actually a proven way to start managing stress levels and allows us to feel better than we may have felt in a long time. **Messy homes can sometimes reflect a messy state of mind, so cleaning the home can also affect the state of mind. It works both ways.**

Another thing you can do to reduce worry is to start using a budget. A budget seems like it's very boring and difficult, but it is a great way for us to start feeling more in control of our lives and paying attention to our finances. It's easy to set up a budget, and once you do so you will begin to feel more relieved by knowing where your time and money goes and not having to worry about whether or not you have some kind of obligation that you need to pay in order to begin feeling in control of the situation at hand.

New hobbies can be a great way to manage your time if you have a lot of anxiety or worries. Sometimes we just have too much time on our hands to overthink situations that don't need to be thought about. Instead of filling up all of your time by thinking and worrying and stressing out, you could instead give yourself an opportunity for distraction by starting a new hobby.

Something that you can do with your hands is always the best call when you are trying to abolish worry from your life, but anything would do as well.

Sometimes, meditation has been known to help us to reduce stress and anxiety. If you are able to maintain a strict meditation schedule, you will find yourself being able to relax and feel more mindful and present within your own life. If it seems too difficult for you to meditate, don't worry. All you really have to do is sit down and be quiet for a while, allowing your thoughts to come and pass and simply acknowledge that they are there. Anybody can do that. It helps us to clear our minds so that we can begin to process our emotions and balance out our perspectives. It is actually a very great step in thinking positively, and it can help us to keep ourselves in touch with what is truly important to us.

Sometimes what is really stopping us from enjoying ourselves is our fear. Worrying too much about the future can really inhibit us in the here and now. Most people who have a hard time with taking risks do so because they are worried or scared. If you are too worried to take a risk, you are going to have to learn eventually that there is no easy way to get amazing things accomplished. You are going to have to take risks and do your best to move forward in your life. If you can't take a risk, then it's going to be very difficult for you to be happy. Sometimes you have to go the way that you are not comfortable with before you can start to combat your own anxiety and worries about other people's perceptions of you or your ability to take the plunge into something that seems unfamiliar.

One of the things that you can do is to take a risk that you never would have expected yourself to take. For example, you can go skydiving or do something else that is equally extraordinary. Something that you never thought you would be able to do in 1 million years. You can start to change your style or do anything that you think might surprise people. If you know it would surprise somebody because they don't expect you to take the risk, you might as well give it a try and see how you like it. Not only will it cause people to have more respect for you, but it will also help you to have more respect for yourself and to feel better about taking risks and less worried about the danger that these risks might entail.

New hobbies can be a great way to manage your time if you have a lot of anxiety or worries. Sometimes we just have too much time on our hands to overthink situations that don't need to be thought about. Instead of filling up all of your time by thinking and worrying and stressing out, you could instead give yourself an opportunity for distraction by starting a new hobby. Something that you can do with your hands is always the best call when you are trying to abolish worry from your life, but anything would do as well. You can start reading new books or even writing books. You could work with your hands and build things or craft things or draw. There are many opportunities for you to take yourself out of your mind and distract yourself from needless worries and empty space that can cause you to begin to catastrophize things.

If you want to stop worrying, you really need to start thinking about slimming down your workload. A lot of worries often feel this way because you have a lot of responsibilities to deal with. If you are feeling overwhelmed by the amount of responsibility that you have to deal with in your own life or your own home, you are going to have to figure out a way that you can balance out these responsibilities. For example, is there somebody that you can turn to and tell them that you have too much on your plate and you are feeling too overwhelmed by these responsibilities?

If you can find somebody and divide up the labor so that you don't feel so overwhelmed by everything that you are doing, all you have to do sometimes is to ask for help and your life will feel that much better. Many times people will surprise you with their willingness to help you out, so never assume that other people don't care about your stress. **Let them know honestly how you are feeling and allow yourself some opportunities to avoid responsibility and give yourself a chance to relax.**

Too much worry and stress can lead to a lot of complications that can actually be bad for your mental health, so never be afraid to ask for help when you need it. Remember that you have more control over your life than you think, and for those times that you cannot have control, you will have to allow yourself to let it go.

There is no shame in not being able to control every aspect of your life, nobody can do that and most people are doing a lot poorer of a job than it looks like.

Try never to judge yourself or compare yourself to other people.

Worrying about other people's achievements and comparing them to your own is the fastest track to unhappiness that there is. In order to stay happy, you have to stay focused on your own goals and achievements, and trust yourself to do what is best for you and every given situation. You know exactly what you need in order to be happy, so trust your instincts and follow your heart so that you can figure out exactly what is true for your life in order to stay positive and focused on achieving the goals that are the most important to your happiness.

Chapter 14 – How To Believe In Yourself

Believing in yourself is one of the most difficult things for anybody to do. Most of us have a very critical inner voice telling us that we are not good enough and that we are never going to accomplish the things that we think we would like to. All of us are much more prone to self-doubt then we are to confidence, whether this is because of society, our upbringing, or our own inner monologue. Whether being confident in yourself is easy for you or difficult, the chances are high that you will need some advice on how to stay focused on a true belief in your ability to succeed.

A great place to begin is to believe that despite our inhibitions and discomfort with extending ourselves to accomplish the goals that we want to accomplish, we are definitely going to move forward in our lives and achieve exactly what we need in order to thrive. In order to believe in ourselves enough to give us the motivation we need to succeed, we have to provide ourselves with the basic foundation to push past whatever difficulties we are feeling and the discomfort of knowing that we may fail despite our best efforts. **Each of us is capable of accomplishing many things with our minds and our brains, but if we are not willing to put ourselves out there for even**

just a moment, we will accomplish nothing.

Something we really have to understand is that it is okay if we never succeed the first time. <u>It is even okay if we don't succeed the second or third time.</u> What makes a failure is if we stop and we give up trying to learn something that is difficult for us. Most people are taught to believe that if they don't get something right the first time, there is something inherently wrong with them. We are not taught how to learn or keep our minds open to constant progression. We do not know how to keep trying and we are always criticizing ourselves for doing something wrong even though we should have no reason to be able to do it right in the first place. We don't allow ourselves the necessary time we need to adapt to a new situation or concept, and so often times the results are half-baked and inconclusive or impossible to follow through with.

Sometimes we lose our confidence halfway through, and stop doing anything that is associated to the project that we were attempting in the first place. We feel so humiliated by our potential failure that we don't even achieve the bragging rights of finishing.

If this sounds familiar to you, don't worry. Almost everybody goes through something similar. All of us believe that we should be better than what we are. When this comes into play and it starts to affect your confidence however, you are going to have to keep a realistic mindset. **You need to learn how to learn,** and allow yourself to believe that your goals are reasonable and they are worth the accomplishment and the work that it would take to get them completed. You have to make sure that you are willing to ignore the negative self-speaking that you do to yourself that sabotages you along the way.

You have to remember and keep in mind that no matter what, you are only failing if you are not

finishing. Failure is not what happens when you finish a project. Even if the project doesn't go as well as you intended, at least you followed it through. **That is something that most people are never able to do, which is why they spend their lives sitting around and wondering what they have done and how they have gone wrong in their live**s. They may have started somewhere, but somewhere along the way they lost confidence in their ideals or in their ability to accomplish their ideals.

If you are able to really put yourself out there and understand that there are risks that are worth taking, and that you are not a failure despite what you may think or even what others might think, then you are going to be a lot more likely to succeed at the project that you have in mind. You have to make sure that you plan ahead and you think about every step that it's going to take in order to accomplish your goals realistically. **Don't go into a giant dream without thinking about how you can break that dream down into smaller goals that are reasonable that you can accomplish in a reasonable amount of time.**

Many people think that success needs to happen overnight, and when it doesn't, they stop believing in themselves. That's not the way it works. Accomplishment takes a lot of time and dedication. It doesn't matter how smart you are or how rich you are, if you don't have any follow-through then your project will never get off the ground and you will stop believing in yourself and stop trusting yourself to make the right decisions. Even if your project was brilliant, if you are unable or unwilling to take the risk of completing it, then you will never know for sure just how much you are truly capable of. If something doesn't work out once, do it twice. Repeat that until it does work out and you're happy with the results. Tenacity is the spice of life, and it is the foundation of believing in yourself.

You have to remember that failure is very subjective and if

you do not believe that you are a failure then you never will be. It doesn't matter what anybody says or does or thinks about you. Nothing that you do can be wrong unless you feel that it is wrong, and if you feel that you have done something wrong you really need to examine everything about your plan. Did you plan it well enough? How did you go about the execution of your plan? Did you give yourself the opportunity to try again and again until you succeeded in the way that you wanted to? Did you treat your mistakes as learning experiences and then start again from the top? If you hadn't done these things, or you are listening to yourself saying that you are a failure and you are not worth anything, then you are going to have a much harder time believing in yourself than if you were able to follow the advice outlined in this chapter.

The power of positive thinking is unbelievable, and when you believe in yourself there is nothing that can stop you from achieving the goals you have set for yourself in your mind. Everybody is able and willing to start gathering information and understanding just how the world can start to affect you if you are willing to change your perspective about things. If you are able to start believing that **mistakes are learning opportunities and that you are a little sponge out in the world who is willing and able to glean any type of information that can help you to accomplish your dreams,** then you are going to have a much healthier mindset and you're going to feel very excited to take on every new challenge and opportunity that comes your way.

All you have to do is practice the art of believing in yourself and allowing yourself to make mistakes sometimes. **Don't use the word fail. Use the word learn.** That will help you to change your perspective from being a negative thinker into a positive one, and ultimately that can help you to change your life for the better.

Something we really have to understand is that it is okay if we never succeed the first time. It is even okay if we don't succeed the second or third time. What makes a failure is if we stop and we give up trying to learn something that is difficult for us.

Most people are taught to believe that if they don't get something right the first time, there is something inherently wrong with them. We are not taught how to learn or keep our minds open to constant progression.

Chapter 15 – How to Practice Self-Soothing

Self-soothing is one of the most beneficial practices in positive thinking. If we are having a crisis or we are consumed by negative thoughts, learning how to self-soothe can help us to comfort ourselves and take our minds away from the negativity of the situation so that we can focus more on the positivity. Anxiety and worry can often trigger us into feeling very negatively and having a hard time dealing with other people. Much of the time, self-soothing techniques are overlooked, and only taught when people are not having an easy time dealing with their own emotions. However, self-soothing can be beneficial for anybody, especially when they are very angry or feeling very negative.

The first step in self soothing when you are feeling stressed out and anxious or consumed by negative encircling thoughts, is to allow yourself to believe that there is a better option for you out there. You have to be very kind to yourself and very forgiving for your own mistakes and misjudgments about things. Everybody has a difficult time with their perception, especially when they are thinking negatively. Sometimes we make mistakes when we are being negative and it affects other people badly. If we cannot allow ourselves to let go of these mistakes and forgive ourselves for acting out based on how our brain has been wired to respond to negativity, then we are going to have to encourage ourselves to learn how to do so in order to achieve a more positive frame of mind.

If we cannot self soothe, then it is very unlikely that we are going to be able to move forward in any positive thinking techniques. Sometimes our anxiety can be so overwhelming that we stop seeing things in a rational perspective and we often listen to those negative voices in our mind telling us that we are worthless or that we cannot achieve anything positive with our lives. This kind of thinking is very destructive, and it can cause us to go down a path that is better left untraveled. Many people who have addictions have gone down the wrong road and never learned how to self soothe.

The first thing that you can do is practice mindfulness and giving yourself some kindness. You have to stay present in your own body and imagine something kind or happy or cute that makes you feel happy. It's a very brief exercise that can change your entire state of being. Allowing yourself to shift perspectives and allow the neurons in your brain to realign with different neural pathway than what your brain is used to will bring you into a new state of being that can help you to stop engaging in a negative activity and bring your thoughts around to a positive one so that you can avoid dealing with a negative state of mind that will not be constructive for you.

You can self soothe by telling yourself that you are okay, and that everything is okay, and that everything will turn out for the best despite your opinions on how things should be. You can remind yourself actively that sometimes everything works out whether we understand why or not.

It can help to keep in mind that we are not always in control, and that there are other people in the world who may have needed a situations work out differently than it did. Sometimes people need different things more than we need them, and we have to allow for the possibility that maybe what we thought was the best solution was not the best solution after all. There's always the opportunity of new doors opening up somewhere else, and that even when you are dealing with something that seems impossible to overcome, somehow through sheer willpower and perseverance, we are able to overcome our obstacles and provide ourselves with an even better opportunity than what we thought we might have lost.

You have to remember that you are very important in your own life, and that if you are unable to think positively about yourself, you are going to have a lot of troubles connecting to other people.

If you don't feel good about yourself, eventually other people will sense this and they may not feel very good about you either.

You have to remember that you are very important in your own life, and that if you are unable to think positively about yourself, you are going to have a lot of troubles connecting to other people. **If you don't feel good about yourself, eventually other people will sense this and they may not feel very good about you either.** You have to keep in mind presently as often as possible that you are worth the time that it takes to achieve your goals, and you are worth being treated well and with respect and dignity. You are also worth being loved and cared for.

If you don't remind yourself of this frequently, sometimes it is easy to fall into negative thought patterns where you begin to blame yourself for the problems that you face or you wonder **if other people are angry at you for no reason.**

Stay confident in what you deserve out of life, otherwise you will become a much more reclusive person to does not know how to soothe their high emotional stresses. People who become overwhelmed by their emotions can often act out and be cruel or unkind to other people. **This can cause lifelong regrets for you**, so it is always best to practice self-soothing whether you think you need to or not. Always remember that you should be kind to yourself and that everybody else should be respectful of you as well. That is what you deserve.

Chapter 16: Radical Steps Toward Self-Empowerment Through Positive Thinking

If you are very serious about improving your life and empowering yourself to the power of positive thinking, there are some serious and radical steps that you can take to change your life immediately.

Gratitude Journal

Starting now, you can begin to keep a gratitude journal. When we really force ourselves to sit down and think about the positive things that have happened throughout our day, then we can begin to weigh out how many positive things happen versus the negative. Although the negative things hurt a lot, the positive things are often more abundant and even more powerful than the negative. If we force ourselves to sit down and think about the impact that the positive things have in our day, rather than sitting around and dwelling and feeling as if that negative moment make all the positive moments obsolete, then we will have a much greater chance of empowering ourselves with positive thinking.

Mindfulness

Something that helps a lot of people in a lot of ways is

practicing mindfulness. Mindfulness is a beautiful technique that allows us to stay present in the moment without worrying about the past or the future. If we are able to keep ourselves isolated in the moment, worry about the future and regrets about the past no longer afflict us. Mindfulness is a technique that can be practiced in meditation or even in your daily life.

All you have to do is close your eyes (optional) and focus on the here and now, shutting away anything that might remind you of something negative.

Check Up On You

Most of us know that we should check in on our friends and family to make sure that they are okay and to nurture our relationship with them. **But what many of us don't know is that we should do the same thing with ourselves.** Sometimes we forget that we are also important, and that can make it very difficult for us to move forward with empowering thoughts and positive thinking. Ask yourself how you're feeling and figure out what you think throughout the day so that you can keep yourself on track and interrupt negative thoughts when they occur.

Be Honest

Many of us have a problem with being honest with ourselves about our flaws. We want to believe that we are perfect. However, you have to believe that you are not perfect in order to follow a path of positive thinking that will change your life. You have to acknowledge that there are negative things about life but you have to also keep in mind that these negative things can be changed. If you ignore them and you don't work on them, they tend to stay there and get infected, causing you to have more negativity in your life than you need.

> If we force ourselves to sit down and think about the impact that the positive things have in our day, rather than sitting around and dwelling and feeling as if that negative moment make all the positive moments obsolete, then we will have a much greater chance of empowering ourselves with positive thinking.

Stay Healthy

Staying healthy is one of the most profound ways to impact our thinking. Our brains and our moods are directly affected by our physical health. If you are unable to stay balanced, take a look at your lifestyle and decide what needs to change in order for you to live a healthier and more fulfilling life that can provide you with more opportunities to stay positive and avoid the negative.

Talk Nicely To Yourself

We talked a lot about negative self-talk, but what we didn't talk a lot about was positive self-talk. Keep in mind that you should never speak cruelly to yourself and bully yourself. What you should do instead, is encourage yourself and be forgiving and kind and gentle. Constantly keep in mind your good qualities and recite them to yourself if you forget them or you feel overwhelmed by what you think is negative about you.

Talk To Kind, Supportive People

Instead of talking to toxic people who will affirm your worst suspicions and fears about yourself, surround yourself with people who have a positive and upbeat attitude who will support your positive self-talk and nurture that aspect of yourself. This has a profound impact on everybody, **as humans are social creatures. Choose your friends wisely and make sure that they are the type who will support you when you need it rather than putting you down.**

Conclusion

All around the world, people struggle with negative thinking. Negativity plagues us in all aspects of life, and it can be difficult for us to remember that the positive is there and it is just as important and impacting as the negative. If we are unable to see through the negative aspects of life in order to find the silver lining on the clouds around us, we may end up finding it impossible to move forward and achieve our hopes and dreams. Not only that, but the stress and anxiety can slowly kill us.

All of this is dangerous and can lead us to being very unhealthy and unhappy individuals. If you want to change your life and implement positive thinking, now is the time to start. It is never too soon to improve yourself and work on habits that may help you to improve your life **and change you for the better forever.** All of us want to move forward, none of us are happy to be stuck behind. All you have to do is take the steps and empower yourself today so **that you can live longer, live happier, and stay healthier than ever before with a positive mindset.**

Did you enjoy reading this book?

Please help others find this book by kindly leaving a review.

Thanks in advance

Jennifer N. Smith

Did you enjoy reading this book? Can I ask you a favour?

Thanks for purchasing and reading this book, I really hope you find it helpful.

If you find this book helpful, **please help others find this book by kindly leaving a review.** I love getting feedback from my customers, loved it or hated it! Just Let me know. and I would really appreciate your thoughts.

Thanks in advance

Jennifer N. Smith

This book mentioned about mindfulness and meditation.

If you want to learn more about how to practice mindfulness and meditation, I highly recommend that you check out my meditation book here.

This book will help you realize that the only thing that's holding you back from having a better life is YOU! **You had the key to turn your life around.** By reading this book you will become empowered to take charge of your life and stop playing victim to life's seemingly impossible challenges.

ABOUT THE AUTHOR

For me, the hardest part of being a mom is learning how to manage my own emotions. I yelled at my son, I felt horrible, guilty and so stressed and tired. I started reading lots of self-help books and I have learned a lot.

I want to share what I have learned throughout the years with my readers; I hope my books can help you deal with your day-to-day challenges, and make you feel happy again, you can create a home full of peace and love for the whole family.

Visit my website here for more self-improvement tips and advice:
http://improve-yourself-today.com

46789555R00059

Made in the USA
Middletown, DE
09 August 2017